# CHARLES KELLER

# Belly Laughs!

## ILLUSTRATED BY RON FRITZ

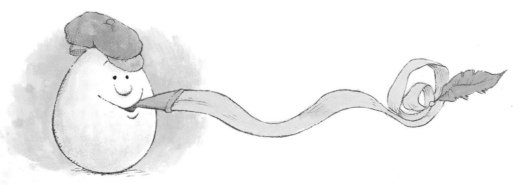

**Simon and Schuster Books for Young Readers**
Published by Simon & Schuster Inc.
New York • London • Toronto • Sydney • Tokyo • Singapore

## SIMON AND SCHUSTER BOOKS FOR YOUNG READERS

Simon & Schuster Building
Rockefeller Center
1230 Avenue of the Americas
New York, New York 10020

SIMON AND SCHUSTER BOOKS FOR YOUNG READERS
is a trademark of Simon & Schuster Inc.

Manufactured in the United States of America

10 9 8 7 6 5 4 3 2 1    (pbk.) 10 9 8 7 6 5 4 3 2 1

*Library of Congress Cataloging-in-Publication Data*
Keller, Charles.   Belly laughs: food jokes & riddles/by
Charles Keller; illustrated by Ron Fritz.
Summary: An illustrated collection of jokes and riddles
with an emphasis on food, including "What's the new
drink for frogs? Croak-a-Cola!"  1. Food—Juvenile
humor.   2. Wit and humor, Juvenile.  [1. Riddles.
2. Jokes.  3. Food—Wit and humor.]  I. Fritz,
Ronald, ill.  II. Title.  PN6231.F66K45  1990
818'.5402—dc20  89-28201
ISBN 0-671-70068-5
ISBN 0-671-70069-3 (pbk.)

Quality Printing by:
ARCATA GRAPHICS/KINGSPORT
Press and Roller Streets
Kingsport, TN 37662   U.S.A.

To Nicole and Leigh
C.K.

To my wife Martha
R.F.

What's the best food to eat
in the bathroom?
Showerkraut!

What kind of cheese is made
in Scotland?
Loch Ness Muenster!

What do anteaters like
on pizza?
Antchovies!

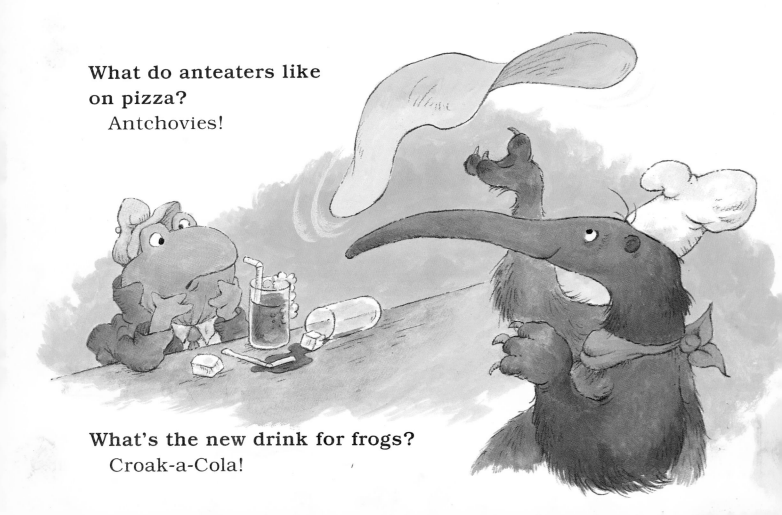

What's the new drink for frogs?
Croak-a-Cola!

What's green, has twenty-two legs, and plays football?
The Green Bay Pickles.

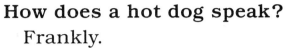

How does a hot dog speak?
Frankly.

What's soft and white and comes from Mars?
Martian-mallows.

What's brown and wrinkled and lives in a church tower?
The Lunch Bag of Notre Dame.

**What did the lettuce say to the celery?**
"Quit stalking me."

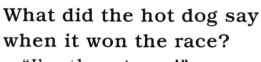

**What did the hot dog say when it won the race?**
"I'm the wiener!"

**What do you get when you cross a pig with a centipede?**
Bacon and legs.

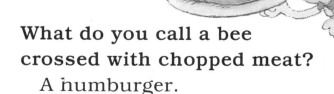

**What do you call a bee crossed with chopped meat?**
A humburger.

**What do you get when you cross a donut and a pretzel?**
A whole new twist.

**What happens when you cross a hamburger and a yo-yo?**
You swallow it—and it comes up again!

**What do ghosts eat for lunch?**
Boo-loney sandwiches!

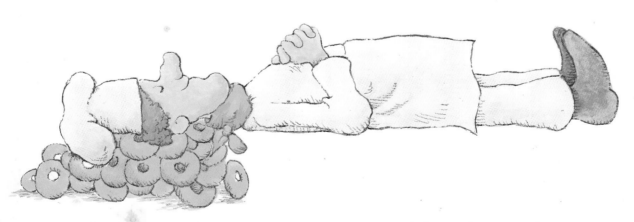

**Why did the baker stop making donuts?**
He was tired of the hole business.

**Why was the manager of the pretzel factory fired?**
He tried to straighten things out.

**Why did the man hold up a slice of bread?**
To propose a toast.

**What kind of sandwich speaks for itself?**
A tongue sandwich.

**How do you make a Mexican chili?**
Take him to the North Pole.

**Where do tough chickens come from?**
Hard-boiled eggs.

**Who writes nursery rhymes
and squeezes oranges?**
Mother Juice.

What did the man say
when they offered
him tapioca?
  "You're pudding me on!"

What did the food say
when it was wrapped up?
  "Curses! Foiled again!"

What do you get when
you stack thousands
of pizzas one on top
of the other?
    The Leaning Tower of Pizza.

What do pizzas ride around on?
    Pie-cycles.

What does the ocean eat for breakfast?
Boatmeal.

What's another name
for white bread?
Ghost toast.

What do you call
hamburger fights?
Meat brawls.

What do ants use for hula hoops?
Cheerios.

What kind of salad do horses eat?
Colestraw.

**What do you call a mischievous egg?**
A practical yolker.

**When does a hot dog wear a coat?**
When it's a chilly dog.

**Which knight ate meat
at every meal?**
Sir Loin.

**What do you say to rotten lettuce?**
"You should have your head examined."

**What do you call a spinach that insults a farmer?**
A fresh vegetable.

**What do you call an all-night Chinese restaurant?**
Wok around the clock.

**What kind of cake holds water?**
Sponge cake.

**What do you call a
small hot dog?**
A teeny wienie.

**Who's long and skinny
and beats a drum?**
Yankee Noodle.

**What does an umpire do before he eats?**
He brushes off his plate.

**What do you get when you squeeze the curtains?**
Drape juice.

**Where do burgers dance?**
At the meat ball.

What do you get when
you pour hot water
down a rabbit hole?
Hot cross bunnies.

What do you call a plate that tells lies?
Dish-honest.

Why did the pirate put a chicken where he
buried the treasure?
Because eggs marks the spot.

What do you call a knife that cuts four loaves of bread at a time?

A four-loaf cleaver.

**What's a pickle?**

A cucumber that turned sour after a jarring experience.

**What's a rotisserie?**

A ferris wheel for chickens.

**What's a daffy dill?**

A crazy pickle!

**What do you call
a stolen yam?**
  A hot potato!

**What do you call a chef
on strike?**
  A cook-out!

What do you call a stolen sausage?
The missing link!

What do you call a
sunburned stomach?
Pot roast!

**What does a waiter bring you after a bison steak?**
A buffalo bill.

**What do you call somebody who works behind a soda counter?**
A fizzician.

**What does a tightrope-walker eat?**
A balanced diet.

What do you get when you
cross Frankenstein's
monster with a hot dog?
Frankfurterstein!

What's Dracula's favorite snack?
Fangfurters!

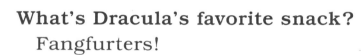

Where do ghosts go for lunch?
Pizza Haunt!

**What do you call a nervous cow?**
 Beef jerky.

**Why did the baby cookie cry?**
 Because her mother was
 a wafer so long.

**How do you make
a hot dog stand?**
 Steal its chair.

**Where do monsters eat?**
At a beastro.

**What do you get when you tell food jokes?**
Belly laughs!

**What happened when they opened
a restaurant on the moon?**
It lacked atmosphere.